FROM FINLAND TO NIAGARA FALLS

Explorer Pehr Kalm in North America
1748 – 1751

Written by Markku Löytönen
Illustrated by Riikka Jäntti
Translated by Christina Saarinen

BUFFALO

HERITAGE

UNLIMITED

Buffalo Heritage Press
266 Elmwood Avenue, Suite 407
Buffalo, NY 14222
www.BuffaloHeritage.com

Originally published in Finnish as *Uutta maailmaa tutkimassa: Tutkimusmatkaaja Pehr Kalm Pohjois-Amerikassa* by SKS in Finland.

Published by

BUFFALO
HERITAGE
UNLIMITED

Buffalo Heritage Press
266 Elmwood Avenue, Suite 407
Buffalo, NY 14222
www.BuffaloHeritage.com

Buffalo Heritage Press gratefully acknowledges the financial assistance of

FINNISH
LITERATURE
EXCHANGE

ISBN: 978-1-942483-13-7 (softcover)
ISBN: 978-1-942483-14-4 (hardcover)
Library of Congress Control Number available upon request

Printed in the United States of America

FOREWORD

Both Europe and North America were very different places in the middle of the eighteenth century when Finnish explorer Pehr Kalm set out for the New World. Kalm was born in the Kingdom of Sweden in 1716. His family was from Finland, the eastern portion of the kingdom. Finland remained a part of Sweden until 1809 and finally became independent in 1917, after a century of Russian rule.

In 1748, when Kalm set sail for North America, the New World had been settled by colonists from many different countries, including Sweden. New Sweden had been established in 1638 in the area where Wilmington, Delaware, now stands. In 1682, the area where the Swedes had settled was incorporated into the British colony of Pennsylvania.

At the time of Kalm's journey, the British colonies were well-established and Philadelphia had already developed into a prosperous city. However, for Europeans, the continent was still a largely unexplored wilderness. Relations with the neighboring French colonies and Native American tribes were often violent. Only a few years after Kalm's visit, the French and Indian War erupted, and Great Britain and France battled for dominance in the New World. The frontier regions where Kalm traveled were very unstable, and Kalm was often in grave danger.

Kalm undertook his dangerous journey in North America to research the plants and animals of the New World. Like other great explorers of his time, however, Kalm did not merely describe the plants and animals but also recounted everything he witnessed, including the people and their customs. He took careful notes, and when he returned to Europe, he published his diaries. The diaries were popular with readers at the time and continue to be an important source of information about the nature and customs of North America in the eighteenth century.

LINNAEUS, A SCIENTIST FOR SWEDEN

Looking back, the centuries of exploration and research expeditions seem full of brazen adventures. However, these journeys were actually motivated by economic and political goals. By the time of the Age of Exploration and the discovery of America, it was clear that conquering lands across the ocean would increase trade and strengthen the position of the mother country in the Old World. So, more and more European nations sent ships sailing over the seas and expeditions into the wilderness to claim land and establish colonies.

By the 1600s, Sweden had established itself as a great European power with an aggressive foreign policy. Its position collapsed in the early 1700s, however, when the Great Northern War with Russia ended in a devastating defeat. Sweden then decided to increase its wealth and the wellbeing of the Swedish people through peace, rather than by conquering land in continental Europe.

The ideas of the Age of Reason were spreading in Sweden, leading people to seek valuable goods through science, education, and trade, rather than through war. When the Royal Academy of Sciences was established in Stockholm in 1739, it was not only scientists but also factory owners and merchants, who were involved.

One of the founders of the Royal Academy of Sciences was the world famous natural scientist Carl Linnaeus. He earned his reputation by devising a taxonomy, a system for the organization of species based on the concept that each of the world's animals, plants, insects, and other living things could be defined as unique species. He believed that the relationships between different species could be discovered by collecting and studying samples of each species. Many natural scientists headed out on research trips to different parts of the world to collect samples of as yet unknown species.

Linnaeus himself did not go on any expeditions. Instead, he sent his students on trips to faraway lands. Some were scientists from Finland, and of these the most famous was Pehr Kalm, who traveled to North America.

Twinflower
Linnea borealis

PEHR KALM

Pehr Kalm was born in March 1716, the son of a priest. His family lived in Ångermanland in Sweden, where they were refugees from Russian-occupied Finland. When the war ended, the family returned home to Finland. Kalm went to school in Vasa and started university studies at the Academy of Turku in 1735. From there, Kalm moved to Uppsala University in Sweden, where a year later he met and became friends with Carl Linnaeus. Under Linnaeus's influence,

Kalm became interested in botany and especially in its applications to farming and industry.

Kalm was a talented student, and it was clear to Linnaeus that Kalm should take part in one of the research expeditions that Linnaeus was planning. Kalm was enthusiastic about the idea and started to carefully prepare for the task. In addition to his studies, Kalm practiced field research on trips to Karelia, to the southwest coast of Sweden, and to

Moscow. The scientific reports that Kalm wrote on these trips convinced Linnaeus of Kalm's skills.

Kalm was ready to travel, but what would be the destination of his expedition? It seemed no one was sure. At first there was talk of a trip to the southernmost point of Africa, the Cape of Good Hope. Next came the idea that Kalm should travel to Greenland, then Siberia was considered.

Finally, Linnaeus's opinion sealed the deal: Kalm would be sent to North America. Kalm himself was satisfied with the decision, since he was eager to get going—for him, the destination didn't make much difference.

A letter from Kalm, just turned thirty years old, to the secretary of the Academy of Sciences, April 1746.

"My youth is running out; it is precisely at this age when everything pleases the eye, and nothing refreshes the mind so much as pondering the phenomena of Nature and the collection of natural artifacts; an unknown herb, an insect which I have never seen before, a new use for some natural artifact can give me more pleasure than a pauper would feel discovering a treasure."

WHY AMERICA?

The Age of Exploration had seen Spain, Portugal, France, and Holland establish colonies all over the world. Colonists had built harbors and cities, which were growing steadily. Ships departed for the mother countries carrying spices, wood, furs, and other riches. Trade flourished and the mother countries grew rich.

Unlike the other great powers of Europe, Great Britain had practiced a cautious foreign policy. Great Britain was afraid of the economic and military advantages held by the nations of continental Europe and had not claimed any territory or established colonies. The success that other countries were enjoying with territories abroad was tempting, however, and little by little Great Britain's foreign policy changed. Great Britain's war with Spain and the defeat of the Spanish Armada in 1588 paved the way for change.

France became the great power of continental Europe instead of Spain, leading France into ongoing conflicts with Great Britain. These conflicts reached their peak between 1754 and 1763, in the French and Indian Wars, which were fought in North America. The winner, Great Britain, became the world's greatest colonial power. The Union Jack waved on all the seas, and the sun never set on the British Empire.

Kalm's trip took place just before the French and Indian Wars broke out. Though North America was technically at peace, in actuality it was a very unstable place, with constant conflicts between French and British troops. The Native Americans were also drawn into the conflict, because the French and British recruited them to support their armies. Bloody revenge raids and kidnappings were everyday occurrences all over the frontier—precisely where Kalm was headed on his expedition.

However, there were excellent scientific reasons for Kalm's journey. The immense North American continent had hardly been studied at all by natural scientists. There were only a few universities, and even these did not encourage research. Trade with the mother country was more important. Hobbyists in the natural sciences could be found here and there, but they were of little help in Linnaeus's quest for information about the plants and animals of the New World.

TO NORWAY AND GREAT BRITAIN

After a long wait and careful preparation, Kalm finally boarded a ship and sailed first to the coast of Norway. Kalm's faithful assistant, Lars Jungström, joined him on the journey. Kalm had just been named a professor, and his trip was sponsored by the Academy of Sciences, which provided him with travel funds and letters of recommendation. At that time, these letters were just as important as passports are today; without them, a visitor to the cities and forts of a dangerous region would be met with suspicion.

From Norway, the trip continued to London, the capital of Great Britain. A stop in London was essential for many reasons. While Great Britain had long practiced cautious foreign policy and had been slow to occupy new territories, it exerted formidable power in the field of research expeditions. British ships and expeditions had for centuries systematically mapped the globe. The reports of these travels were archived in London's libraries, and the animal, plant and insect specimens that had been brought back were found in the city's many museums and botanical gardens.

Kalm spent a productive six months in London studying the literature and becoming thoroughly acquainted with the information available about the New World. Kalm also met many other natural scientists and spoke with people who had traveled in North America. He learned to speak both English and French, since he planned to visit both British and French areas. And before he set sail, Kalm collected letters of recommendation from well-known London natural scientists.

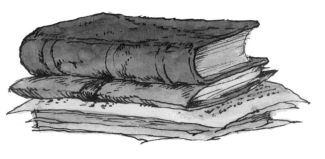

"Kalm spent half a year in England . . . and took notes on everything he learned about England's natural environment, economy, and people. His travel diary includes more than three hundred hefty pages concerning England alone."
Anto Leikola 1990

FULL SPEED OVER THE ATLANTIC

Finally, the day arrived when Kalm and his assistant set out on their real expedition. The years of studying natural science, practicing fieldwork, learning languages, and preparing for the conditions of the North American continent were over. Now, they faced the journey by sea across the Atlantic Ocean.

In August 1748, Kalm climbed aboard the ship *Mary Galley* in Gravesend. The ship was unmoored, the sails were raised, and the bow was turned westward. The ship's captain was an experienced sailor who explained that the trip to Philadelphia typically took fourteen weeks during the winter. Bad winds, however, could make the journey take as long as nineteen weeks. Even though it was only late summer when the ship set sail, the travelers expected to be riding the waves for a long time.

Luck was on their side, however. The weather was good for the entire trip, and the winds were, for the most part, favorable and strong, without being stormy. The trip went smoothly and they reached Delaware Bay in record time: the trip took forty-one days, just short of six weeks.

10

During the final days before reaching Philadelphia, the ship sailed along the Delaware River. The first mate on the ship was from Philadelphia, and he showed Kalm the settlements along the river where Finns or Swedes lived. When at last the ship docked, a large crowd of townspeople gathered, looking for letters from their relatives in the Old World.

From Kalm's Diary, June 15, 1748

"Letters of recommendation are not only useful, but essential for those who travel in foreign lands. With the help of letters, the traveler is soon known, liked, and trusted. How could one otherwise trust anyone who has never been seen or heard of before?"

IN THE NEW WORLD

On September 15, 1748, Kalm and Jungström set foot for the first time in the New World. They took leave of the ship's crew and other passengers whom they had gotten to know during the journey and set off for the city with the ship's captain. The letters of recommendation were a tremendous help, and they were welcomed warmly and offered help with finding lodging.

After exploring the city, Kalm decided to set up base for his expeditions in the local settlement of Swedes and Finns. He rented rooms from a small merchant, one for himself and a second for his assistant, and arranged for meals, firewood, and laundry service at a reasonable price. This became his home for three and a half years, except for those times when he was traveling inland.

Kalm thought that Philadelphia was an excellent place for a home base. At that time, Philadelphia was the continent's second largest city after Boston. The harbor was bustling with travelers and served both sea and inland routes. The surrounding countryside was settled widely, if sparsely. Food was available at a good price at the markets, and other supplies could be acquired from the many large and small shops. The city's craftsmen were highly skilled and could produce to order anything that was needed. All in all, Kalm was well satisfied with his lodging and the prosperous city.

From Kalm's Diary, September 16, 1748

"Everyone who acknowledges God to be the Creator, preserver, and ruler of all things, and teaches or undertakes nothing against the state, or against the common peace, is at liberty to settle, stay, and carry on his trade here, be his religious principles ever so strange. No one is here molested on account of the erroneous principles of the doctrine which he follows if he does not exceed the above-mentioned bounds."

Mountain laurel
Kalmia latifolia

KALM'S NAMESAKE - A STATE FLOWER

The moment Kalm stepped off the ship he realized he was entering an entirely new world of plants. Everywhere he looked, his well-trained eye fell upon plants he didn't recognize. As he walked, he stopped constantly to ask the English and Swedish names of unfamiliar plants.

Of all types of plants, Kalm was most interested in grasses. As fate would have it, the very first new plant that he came across in the New World was the grass plant sorghum. As Kalm examined the sorghum plant, he wondered how he would ever accomplish the massive task ahead of him; there were certainly thousands of unknown plants on the continent. During his trip, Kalm collected and dried a huge number of plant varieties, which he shipped to Linnaeus for categorization. Kalm did not define any new genera or species, instead leaving that task to Linnaeus.

Geographical places like islands, bays or straits have traditionally been named after famous explorers. For example, the Bering Strait, which divides the Eurasian and North American continents, is named after the Danish explorer Vitus Bering. In the same way, it is a special honor for a scientist to have his or her name used when a Latin scientific name is created for a new plant or animal species.

Kalm hoped that Linnaeus would name some bush or plant from North America after him. And Linnaeus did just that sometime shortly before his death, giving the Latin name *Kalmia latifolia* to the mountain laurel. The flower is well known in the United States, where it has become the state flower of both Pennsylvania and Connecticut.

Robert geranium
Geranium robertianum

Sorghum
Sorghum vulgare

From Kalm's Diary, September 20, 1748

"A species of Rhus [Rhus vernix L.], *which is common in the marshes here, is called the poison tree by both English and Swedes. . . . I have known old people who were more afraid of this tree than of a viper; and I was acquainted with a person who, merely by the noxious exhalations of it, was swelled to such a degree, that he was as stiff as a log of wood."*

Northern mockingbird
Mimus polyglottus

DEFENSE OF THE SKUNK

Even though Kalm specialized in botany, his task was to observe all of North America's nature and inhabitants as comprehensively as possible. Therefore, Kalm recorded in his notes and diaries observations of plants, animals, and insects, as well as people and their customs.

On his travels in North America, Kalm found a great number of animals that he had never seen before. For example, there were many varieties of squirrels, various small and large mammals, many varieties of birds, and above all, a huge number of snakes, which were feared because they were poisonous.

One new animal that lived only in the New World was the skunk, which has an effective defense strategy against its enemies: the skunk's urine is so repulsively smelly that it sends any attacker running.

Northern flying squirrel
Glaucomys sabrinus

Common mullein
Verbascum thapsus

The meat of the skunk, however, is delicious, and it was used for food by both the Native Americans and the colonists.

Kalm experienced the stink of a skunk first hand when one came close to a house where he was staying. A sheep had died near the house, which apparently attracted the skunk. When the house's dogs went after the skunk, it defended itself by spraying the dogs. The dogs retreated immediately, as did the skunk—but the awful smell lingered around the house for a long time.

From Kalm's Diary, November 3, 1748

"the stink [from the skunk] was so extremely great that, though I was at some distance, it affected me in the same manner as if I had been stifled; and it was so disagreeable to the cattle that it made them roar very loudly: however, by degrees it vanished."

Striped skunk
Mephitis mephitis

WINTER IN PHILADELPHIA

Long into the autumn, Kalm continued his work searching for new species in the region around Philadelphia. As fall turned to winter, however, Kalm could no longer research plants in the field. Instead, Kalm met with the natural scientists of the city, spent time in the Swedish and Finnish settlements, and became familiar with the culture of the New World. At the same time, he prepared for the following summer's journey, his first months-long trek, which would lead deep into French Canada.

Kalm was a sharp-eyed observer and noted objects and customs that were different than those he was accustomed to in Europe. He found the local people to be hard working and orderly. Homes were clean and in good condition. There was plenty of food, and in the summer, berries and fruit were carefully preserved for the winter. The social life of the city was active, even during the winter, and Kalm got to know others who had recently moved from Europe, as well as people whose families had lived in the New World for several generations.

One of Kalm's many visits to the homes of local residents stood out from the others. In March 1749, as winter was finally beginning to break, Kalm set

out to meet ninety-one-year-old Nils Gustafson to ask about New Sweden, the first settlement of Swedes and Finns in North America. Gustafson had been one of its early settlers, and despite his age, he was still sharp and had a good memory.

Kalm learned many things from the old man. The first residents had brought livestock with them. In the New World their herds grew so large that they were able to sell cattle, horses, chickens, sheep, and other domesticated animals to those who arrived after them. They also brought seed from their home country, which was sown for the first harvest once the fields had been cleared. The settlers had gotten along well with the Dutch as well as with the English, who arrived later. At first, the settlers had preserved the customs of their home country, but over time they had also adopted customs from settlers who had come from other countries.

From Kalm's Diary, September 22, 1748

"I met with people here who maintained that giants had formerly lived in these parts, and the following particulars confirmed them in this opinion. A few years ago some people digging in the ground, met with a grave which contained human bones of an astonishing size. . . . Among the savages . . . there is an account . . . that in this neighborhood, on the banks of a river, there lived a very tall and strong man, in ancient times, who carried the people over the river on his back, and waded in the water, though it was very deep."

INDIANS AND SLAVES

When describing the species of the New World, Kalm often includes the Native American names and uses for the plants and animals. However, Kalm notes that in the English colonies of the East Coast, it was possible to go six months without seeing a Native American, because they had been pushed inland as Europeans settled the coast.

As Kalm's travels expanded beyond Philadelphia and into unsettled areas and French Canada, his contact with American Indian tribes increased. In Canada, Kalm mentions Indians of various tribes in the cities, as well as the brisk trade between the French and the Indians. He makes detailed notes on Indian food, clothing, dwellings, and tools. When traveling in areas not settled by Europeans, Kalm was often afraid of Indian attack.

Raccoon
Procyon lotor

Purple martin
Progne subis

While Kalm mentions Native Americans extensively throughout his diaries, his description of Blacks in America is much more limited. Kalm describes slavery and Blacks in America along with the other kinds of labor used in the colonies: free servants and indentured servants. Free servants were hired a year at a time and could leave their work at any time. Indentured servants came from Germany, England, Ireland, and other European countries, but didn't have the money to pay for their trip to the New World. When they arrived, they sold themselves for several years to an employer, who paid the ship captain the cost of their journey. Kalm explains that indentured servants were the most affordable type of labor.

At the time of Kalm's trip to Philadelphia, the slave trade brought Blacks from Africa first to the Caribbean and then to North America. Kalm tells that slaves were bought by almost everyone who could afford them, although some people believed that slavery was immoral, and some freed their slaves—which was, however, a very expensive process.

Wigwam

Kalm's descriptions of non-Europeans are influenced by the prejudices and ignorance of his time. However, he remains true to his research mission of simply describing the people and natural environment of the New World and does not offer any opinion on the issues of conflicts between Europeans and Native Americans or the slave trade.

From Kalm's Diary, December 6, 1748

"The Negroes or Blacks make the third kind [of servants in the English American colonies]. They are in a manner slaves; for when a Negro is once bought, he is the purchaser's servant as long as he lives, unless he gives him to another, or makes him free. However it is not in the power of the master to kill his Negro for a fault, but he must leave it to the magistrates to proceed according to the laws."

WITHIN SHOOTING DISTANCE OF DEATH

In 1749, as summer arrived, Kalm departed with his assistant and two English guides on his first long trek northward. The plan was to travel by foot, paddling, and rowing, into French Canada, through Montreal and Quebec, all the way to Cap-aux-Oies (Goose Cape), about seventy-five miles northeast of Quebec. The trip continued smoothly as weeks and months passed. Kalm found new plants, took notes on all he observed, and enjoyed himself. The letters of recommendation he carried opened doors both at settlements and at the carefully guarded forts along the way. Kalm and his companions were received with exceptional hospitality and provided with advice and supplies for the next leg of the journey.

Once, having traveled five days from the last fort, Kalm's group came upon the remains of a campfire in the middle of the immense, uninhabited forest. The cinders still glowed red. The group that had been there before them had continued onwards only a short time earlier. Kalm was disappointed because he would have liked to have met another group of travelers—it was very rare to cross paths with other people outside of villages and forts.

They didn't find anyone in the area, however, so Kalm and the others continued their trip to the next rest stop. But at the end of their day's travel, they unexpectedly came across a French officer and five soldiers, who were accompanying three Englishmen home.

Kalm told them about the smoldering remains of the fire. The soldiers grew afraid and told Kalm and his companions that they had been within shooting distance of death. Six Indians from French territory had gone out on a revenge raid and passed their fort five days earlier. The group was on its way to kill a white Englishman as revenge for the death of the brother of one of the Indians. Kalm's group continued on its way and made it to a nearby fort.

From Kalm's Diary, June 23, 1749

"During the last war, which had just ended, the inhabitants retreated from [the village] to Albany because the French Indians had taken or killed all the people they met with, set the houses on fire, and cut down the trees. Therefore, when the inhabitants returned they found no houses and were forced to lie under a few boards which were huddled together."

American bullfrog
Rana catesbeiana

White-tailed deer
Odocoileus virginianus

A CRY FROM THE RIVER

Kalm and his companions rested at the fort for several days and replenished their supplies. On the last evening, they packed the provisions they had received from the fort and prepared to continue their trip the following morning. The group had just sat down to dinner with the commander of the fort when they heard a terrible scream from the direction of the river. The commander knew that the sound meant bad news; the group of Indians that had spent the night at the campfire had succeeded.

Kalm went quickly to the window and saw the Indians' boat approaching. The group had left the campfire and made their way to a colonists' settlement, where they found a man mowing a field with his nine-year-old son. The Indians had quietly sneaked closer and, in one fell swoop, killed the man, beheaded him, and kidnapped the boy. They divided up and put on pieces of the father's clothing.

As the boat approached the shore, Kalm could make out the dead man's head hanging from the Indians' spear. He could also see the frightened boy. The Indians were taking him back to their tribe to replace the brother who had been killed in a conflict. When they landed ashore, the Indians sang and danced to celebrate their successful raid.

From Kalm's Diary, July 5, 1749

"The son of the murdered man had nothing but his shirt, breeches and cap, and the Indians had marked his shoulders with red [paint]."

The commander of the fort didn't dare interfere in the events, even though peace had been negotiated and revenge raids were strictly forbidden. Weeks later, when the group of Indians arrived in Montreal, the French governor of the city reprimanded them harshly and took custody of the boy so that he could be returned to his home with the English.

North American beaver
Castor canadensis

LOST

Despite what he had seen, Kalm continued his journey deep into the wilderness. At times, the rivers were so full of beaver dams and fallen trees that the travelers feared the birch bark boat they had built would be damaged. At other times, the current was so strong that it was safer to take the boat and supplies on their shoulders and continue onward by foot.

At a fork in the river, the group decided to take the branch with the weaker current in the hope of being able to travel by boat as far as possible. It was exhausting to carry the boat and supplies, and they were typically covering tens of miles every day. The travelers were happy to find that they were able to travel by boat on the peaceful river for the entire day.

As night was falling, Kalm looked at the reeds in the river and, to his dismay, realized that they had been traveling against the current. This meant the whole day's trip had been a waste because they were going in the wrong direction. The boat was turned around and they hastily started to head back. Night fell quickly, however, and the travelers decided to spend the night on a small island in the middle of the river.

From Kalm's Diary, July 1, 1749

"At day break we got up, and rowed a good while before we got to the place where we left the true road."

Eastern white pine
Pinus strobus

The night was anything but restful. There were so many mosquitoes that no one got any sleep. Kalm and his companions didn't dare to light a fire to keep the mosquitoes away because they were afraid of being discovered by the Indians in the area. They were even more afraid when they heard the barking of the Indians' dogs echoing in the night.

NIAGARA FALLS

From Goose Cape, Kalm and his group had planned to continue traveling north. The commander of the fort forbade them from traveling further, however, because the frontier was still too dangerous after the recent conflicts. Disappointed, Kalm turned towards home, determined to travel to Niagara Falls the following summer.

Kalm's second long expedition started along the same route as the first, following the Delaware River. Just beyond Albany, however, the group turned west and began a weeks-long journey through the territory of the feared Iroquois Indians towards the fort near the falls. The trip went smoothly, and Kalm and his companions arrived safely at Fort Niagara.

According to rumors, Niagara Falls was massive. Those who had seen the falls described mist billowing high up into the air and the roar of the water which, in calm weather, they said could be heard ten miles away. But not a single natural scientist had researched the falls first hand and reported their findings.

Early on the morning of July 24, Kalm set out for the falls accompanied by three French officers and three soldiers. Along the way, Kalm was able to see and hear for himself that the stories about the falls were true. From a long way off, the mist which rose towards the sky gleamed in the bright sunshine. It was like a giant pillar of smoke, which slowly bent in the gentle breeze. The thunder of the falls reached Kalm's ears hours before he arrived at the waterfall.

When Kalm finally reached the edge of the falls, he couldn't believe his eyes. An enormous torrent of water a half a mile wide rushed toward a steep cliff, and from there dropped 175 feet to the depths below. The rushing water continued downriver through whirlpools and rapids before it eventually leveled out.

Kalm stared, transfixed by the sight. He then got to work, making a detailed scientific description of the falls. He measured the height and width of the falls and made careful field notes of all he had seen. For some reason, there was an abundance of snakes in the area.

From Kalm's account of Niagara Falls, published in the *Pennsylvania Gazette*, September 20, 1750

"When all this water comes to the very fall, there it throws itself down perpendicular! The hair will rise and stand upright on your head when you see this! I cannot with words express how amazing this is! You cannot see it without being quite terrified; to behold so vast a quantity of water falling headlong from so surprising a height!"

BENJAMIN FRANKLIN, A FAMOUS FRIEND

By the time Kalm arrived in Philadelphia, Benjamin Franklin was already well-known as a scientist, inventor, and statesman. He was famous among the educated people of the New World, and his reputation had carried over to Europe. He was also among the first local natural scientists

Kalm met, offering his precious letters of recommendation for Franklin to examine.

A deep friendship quickly formed between the two men. Kalm was a frequent visitor to Franklin's home, and Franklin introduced Kalm to the most important scientists in the city.

After this, doors opened everywhere for Kalm, and he was quickly accepted by the city's scientific community.

When Kalm returned from his second expedition to Niagara Falls, he showed his field notes and measurements of the falls to Franklin. Franklin asked Kalm to write a report for his newspaper, *The Pennsylvania Gazette,* and Kalm was happy to oblige. The article was published in September 1750, well before Kalm returned home to Finland.

Kalm's article and its illustrations were republished the following January in London by *Gentleman's Magazine,* and the famous natural historian John Bartram quoted the text in his own description of America, which was published in 1751.

Benjamin Franklin's distinguished career continued long after Kalm's visit to America. Only thirty years after Kalm's trip, Franklin helped draft the Declaration of Independence, was one of its first signatories, and later served as the newly independent United States' first ambassador to France.

From Kalm's Diary, June 29, 1749

"Tea is differently esteemed by different people. . . . However, I must be impartial, and mention in praise of tea, that if it be useful, it must certainly be so in summer, on such journeys as mine, through a desert country where the water is generally unfit for use. . . . In such cases, it is very relishing when boiled, and tea is drunk with it; and I cannot sufficiently describe the fine taste it has in such circumstances."

STARTING A FAMILY

While in Philadelphia, Kalm had become familiar with the local Swedish–Finnish congregation. Kalm's father was a priest, and he himself was devoutly religious, participating in worship services whenever possible. Most often he attended the same small church where most of the Swedish and Finnish colonists worshiped.

In early spring 1748, the congregation greeted a new pastor from Sweden, Johan Sandin, along with his wife Anna Margareta Sjöman, a young daughter, and a newborn child. The congregation welcomed the new arrivals, but Sandin's time as the head of the congregation was cut short when he died on September 22 of the same year—only a week after Kalm arrived in Philadelphia.

Sandin's death put the congregation in a difficult position because there was only one Swedish priest in the region, and he was already struggling to care for the needs of his constantly growing congregation. In the winter of 1748–1749, Kalm often assisted the priest at worship services and in other business.

From Kalm's Diary, July 24, 1749

"The women in general are handsome here [in Montreal]; they are well bred, and virtuous, with an innocent and becoming freedom. They dress out very fine on Sundays; and though on the other days they do not take much pains with other parts of their dress, yet they are very fond of adorning their heads."

When he returned from his first long expedition, Kalm spent his second winter in Philadelphia. Over the winter, his friendship with Sandin's widow turned into love—after all, Kalm was at the prime age for marriage by the period's standards. Their courtship resulted in marriage in February 1750. The wedding was celebrated according to Old World traditions, but the feast was prepared from New World foods. Kalm, who had left for America as a bachelor, returned to Finland with a wife and two stepchildren. The couple had many more children together in Finland.

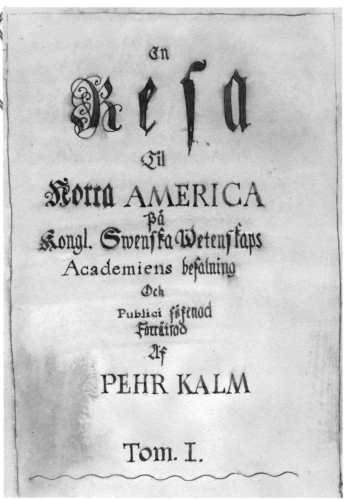

From Jacques Rousseau's Forward to the French Canadian Edition of Kalm's Travelogue

"Everything that he came in contact with while abroad became a topic for research and scientific observation, whether it was human traits, phenomena he discovered, or the elements of nature. He is, however, more of a practical person than a theorist. Largely due to his personality, more so than as a matter of learned tradition, he belongs to that class of universalist natural historians, whom Alexander von Humboldt some years later so brilliantly represented."

BACK IN THE CLASSROOM

Kalm, his family, and his assistant left for Finland a year after the wedding. Their wintry sea journey took the group first to London, then to Gothenburg, and finally through Stockholm to Uppsala, where Kalm finally met with his honored teacher, Linnaeus. Kalm gave an extensive report on his three-and-a-half-year journey, and in August Kalm's family finally traveled to Turku, where a professorship at the academy awaited him.

Kalm spent his first year at the academy on sabbatical writing the first volume of his travelogue. When he began lecturing a year later, the lecture hall was overflowing with eager students. Kalm's lectures on the New World, its plants and animals, its native peoples, colonists and customs, were thrilling to hear in distant Finland in the second half of the 1700s.

Kalm also labored in the garden he established for the seeds he had brought back from North America. He conducted all kinds of experiments to try to determine whether any North American species could be farmed successfully in Sweden and Finland's difficult climate and nutrient-poor land. The results of his experiments were rather lackluster, however. One test after another failed, and the plants did not thrive in Finland. The only species which spread to Finland due to Kalm's efforts is the Virginia creeper, an easily recognizable vine which climbs patiently up the walls of Finnish houses and turns dark red in the autumn.

In addition to his plant experiments, Kalm continued lecturing, wrote additional volumes of his travelogue and served as a pastor. He also advised many students researching North America and dreamed of returning to the New World. The opportunity never arose, however, and Kalm died in Turku in 1779, at the age of 63.

Markku Löytönen is a professor of Human Geography at the University of Helsinki and is well-known in Finland as a popular science author. Among his many publications are five children's books, for which he has received five literature awards.

Riikka Jäntti is an author and illustrator of children's storybooks, novels, and nonfiction. She graduated from the University of Art and Design Helsinki and creates her illustrations with colored markers, gouache, and fairy dust. Her novels have been translated into Japanese, Swedish, and Danish.

Christina Saarinen grew up in Buffalo, New York, not far from Niagara Falls. She has also lived in Turku, Finland, in an apartment overlooking an oak tree said to have grown from an American acorn planted by Pehr Kalm. A graduate of Bryn Mawr College and the University of Helsinki, Christina lives in Buffalo with her husband and son.

REFERENCES

Leikola, Anto. "Valistuksen vuosisadan suomalaisia maailmalla: Kalm, Forsskål, Laxman" [Finns of the Enlightenment Abroad: Kalm, Forsskål, Laxman] In *Matka-arkku – suomalaisia tutkimusmatkailijoita* [Travel Trunk – Finnish Explorers], edited by Markku Löytönen, 8-23. Helsinki: Finnish Literature Society, 1990.

Kalm, Pehr. *Travels into North America: Containing its Natural History, with the Civil, Ecclesiastical and Commercial State of the Country.* Translated by Johann Reinhold Forster. 1770-1771. Reprint, New York: Cambridge University Press, 2011.

CPSIA information can be obtained at www.ICGtesting.com
Printed in the USA
BVIW12n0358140517
483690BV00002B/3